TEEN *Life* SKILLS

Planning for College

Don Nardo

ReferencePoint Press®

San Diego, CA

About the Author

In addition to his many acclaimed volumes about ancient civilizations, historian and award-winning author Don Nardo has published several studies of current social, political, and economic issues, including *The Women's Movement*, *Debates on LGBT Issues*, *Careers in Education*, and *Careers in Film, TV, and Theater*. Nardo, who also composes and arranges orchestral music, lives with his wife, Christine, in Massachusetts.

Picture Credits:
Cover: Monkey Business Images/Shutterstock.com
 6: RyFlip/Shutterstock.com
10: goodluz/Shutterstock.com
12: Syda Productions/Shutterstock.com
17: David Litman/Shutterstock.com
23: TerryJ/iStock
28: David Litman/Shutterstock.com
32: Alex Potemkin/iStock
36: monkey business images/iStock
39: Kaplan Test Prep/Shutterstock.com
44: HaizhanZheng/iStock
48: Associated Press
52: Dan Leone
56: fizkes/Shutterstock.com

LIBRARY OF CONGRESS CATALOGING-IN-PUBLICATION DATA

Name: Nardo, Don, 1947– author.
Title: Planning for College/by Don Nardo.
Description: San Diego, CA: ReferencePoint Press, Inc., 2020. | Series: Teen Life Skills | Audience: Grades: 9 to 12. | Includes bibliographical references and index. |
Identifiers: LCCN 2019011290 (print) | LCCN 2019016796 (ebook) | ISBN 9781682827529 (eBook) | ISBN 9781682827512 (hardback)
Subjects: LCSH: College choice—United States—Juvenile literature. | Campus visits—United States—Juvenile literature. | College costs—United States—Juvenile literature. | College applications—United States—Juvenile literature. | Teenagers—Life skills guides—Juvenile literature.
Classification: LCC LB2350.5 (ebook) | LCC LB2350.5 .N26 2020 (print) | DDC 378.1/61—dc23
LC record available at https://lccn.loc.gov/2019011290

CONTENTS

Why Go to College?

"There are some things college gave me that nothing else would have been able to," says successful educator and videographer Simon Fraser.

No other time in life do you experience maximum freedom and minimum responsibility. Your life is your own, your choices are your own, and you are utterly independent for the first time in your life. You are surrounded by hundreds of people your age who are entering a new stage of their lives, and naturally open themselves up to new ideas. It's such a unique social experience, and you have enough independence to explore it to the fullest extent.[1]

As Fraser did, each year millions of young people leave the experiences of high school behind and go off to college. They expect, or at least hope, that a college education will be a major gateway to adulthood, the world of work, mature responsibilities, and benefits. Going to college is for many people, therefore, a crucial life transition and experience.

Social and Financial Benefits

Fraser recalls how for him attending college was an important social experience in which, for the first time in his life, he was not under the daily supervision of his parents. It was now up to him alone to manage his time and fulfill his daily and weekly obligations. Indeed, many college graduates look back on their time in college as the period when they first established their adult social identities.

Yet although the social aspect of going to college is very real, it is only one of several reasons that college can be a pivotal part of a person's life. Another is the fact that overall, college graduates make more money than people who do not go to college. Of course, nearly everyone knows, or has at least heard of, someone who never went to college but ended up attaining success in life and making lots of money. Hearing about such cases, some people may wonder why it's necessary to go to college. Why bother, they may ask, if one can achieve success without it?

The problem with this viewpoint is that such cases, though real, are quite rare. The few individuals like that—who beat the system through some lucky breaks coupled with hard work—constitute the exception rather than the rule. Derek Thompson, a staff writer for the *Atlantic*, remarks, "Take out that globe [and] give it a spin. I challenge you to land on a region where education gains aren't translating to productivity and income gains." The highest-income countries, he points out, have the most educated populations, which creates more jobs and stronger economies. "There is a cost to not educating young people. The evidence is literally all around us."[2]

> "There is a cost to not educating young people. The evidence is literally all around us."[2]
>
> —Derek Thompson, a staff writer for the *Atlantic*

Some of that evidence takes the form of statistics that show that in general college graduates have a clear financial advantage. Findings collected by the Bureau of Labor Statistics show that people with a bachelor's, or four-year, degree make about 64 percent more per week than individuals with only a high school diploma. Moreover, people with four-year degrees earn roughly 40 percent more than those

For many young adults, college is the first time that they are free to make their own choices and be truly independent. They are exposed to many new ideas and can explore who they are.

with associate's, or two-year, degrees. Similarly, someone with an associate's degree more often than not makes about 17 percent more than someone with only a high school diploma. These percentage differences add up over time. Indeed, comparing the average annual salaries of graduates with bachelor's degrees to those with high school diplomas reveals a difference of nearly $24,000 in annual income.

A Spin of the Globe

Still another important reason to go to college is that doing so can expand one's network of contacts in the professional world. In college, one can meet and get to know talented, ambitious fellow students who aim to eventually succeed in a variety of fields. Properly cultivated, these friends and acquaintances can develop into one's personal network of professional contacts—people one can approach in the future to seek advice, favors, or even employment.

Furthermore, this is the sort of social and professional networking that has for generations helped various college graduates move into pivotal roles as national leaders of various kinds. These individuals range widely from community leaders and technology innovators to Wall Street investors, politicians, artists, and humanitarians. The Hispanic Scholarship Fund, which helps many young Americans pay for college, states:

> A college education is not only important because it leads to higher wages over a lifetime, it also broadens the scope of opportunities available after graduation. A quick look at the backgrounds of today's leaders shows what most of us suspect: college graduates are more likely to attain positions of influence at the local, national, and global levels. Want to lead a city, a county, or the nation? College provides the foundation. Are you interested in helping others? You can have a bigger impact if you've gone to college.[3]

CHAPTER ONE

Thinking Ahead

Probably everyone has either read or heard someone say that nowadays getting into college is not as easy as it once was. The problem with that common adage is that it's largely untrue. The reality is that it only *seems* that way.

Dayeel Dauphine used to be one of those people. The son of Haitian immigrants, he grew up in the small town of Greenacres, Florida, in a single-parent household where money was scarce. "I felt like a lost cause," he recollects. He says that when he was a sophomore in high school in 2015, "college definitely was not on my to-do list." Instead, his goal when he entered high school was just to graduate and "immediately make money."[4] Yet in his freshman year, a teacher recommended that he join a college-preparedness program called AVID. It encouraged him so much that he brought up his grades and started viewing college as a realistic goal. By 2017, when he was a senior, Dauphine had applied to and been accepted by four well-known universities. He ended up at Notre Dame, where he majored in mechanical engineering.

Record Increases in Application Numbers

Dauphine's experience and the experiences of millions of others like him show that getting accepted to college is not beyond reach for most students. Even though it doesn't always feel that way, many colleges actually have a higher acceptance rate now than they did in the past, says Dan Edmonds. Edmonds works for Noodle, an education company that helps high school students and parents with the college search process. In most cases someone who wants to go to college should be able to attend one school or another.

The exceptions, Edmonds explains, are when students apply to a small number of extremely popular schools that receive enormous numbers of applications. Those schools have always been difficult to get into. And now, mainly because each year millions of high school students apply to a much larger number of schools than was common in the past, those schools are even harder to crack. "I'm 43," Edmonds says, "and when I was applying to college, the norm was applying to three or four schools." In contrast, he continues, "today, applying to six or seven places is on the low end. Many high achieving students will apply to 10 or 15 schools, so you're looking at doubling or even tripling the number of applications from the same pool of applicants."[5]

> "[Today] many high achieving students will apply to 10 or 15 schools."[5]
>
> —Dan Edmonds, vice president of research and development for the education company Noodle

The good news, says Greg Daugherty of the nonprofit independent news organization the *Hechinger Report*, is that those colleges (known as elite schools because of their reputations for academic excellence) make up only about 10 percent of the roughly two thousand American colleges and universities. The other 90 percent—or about eighteen hundred schools—have acceptance rates of 50 percent or more. And that number is growing.

The Right High School Courses and Activities

A bit of strategic thinking ahead while still in high school can help a prospective college applicant decide how many and which colleges to apply to, as well as how to prepare for applying. A good place to start is with the question of which high school classes to take, particularly during one's junior and senior years. The fact is that many colleges require that you take certain courses simply to be eligible to apply. For example, if you are interested in going into engineering as a career, you will want to major in engineering in college. So you should investigate whether your high school offers any special courses or programs in engineering, and if so, make sure to take those classes.

In a similar vein, depending on what a person wants to study in college, he or she might want to take some honors or AP (advanced placement) courses, which almost all high schools offer to their more ambitious, hardworking students. Taking such accelerated courses may or may not prepare you better for doing well in college courses later. That mostly depends on how serious you are about studying hard. What is more certain is that taking some advanced classes in high school often looks impressive on one's college application.

Another area of one's high school career to think about is involvement in sports, clubs, music or dramatics programs, and other extracurricular activities. Not only is taking part in such activities fun, it also looks good on a college application. But try to avoid spreading yourself too thin. Some experts say it's actually better to show your ability to commit to and reliably stick with a few pursuits than to take part in dozens of activities and show

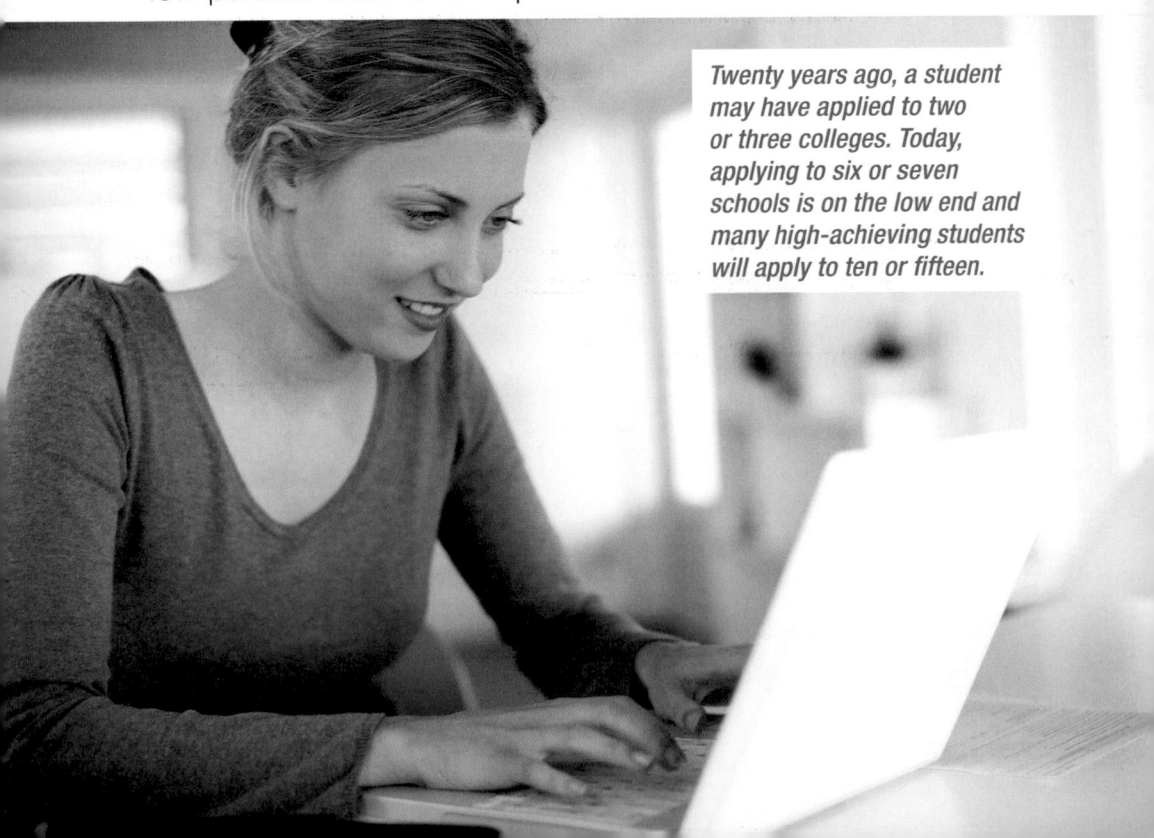

Twenty years ago, a student may have applied to two or three colleges. Today, applying to six or seven schools is on the low end and many high-achieving students will apply to ten or fifteen.

How I Picked My Major When Doing Nothing

Aspiring speech therapist Shayna Heichman graduated from the University of Illinois at Champaign-Urbana in 2018. In her popular blog, she recalls how, as a high school senior, she chose her college major when she least expected it.

> When I was faced with the big decision of picking my major and future career four years ago, I was at a standstill. I had so many interests, [so] how was it possible to pick just one? . . . I planned and thought, and planned some more. But it was when I was on a road trip with my family to Colorado, when I had finally stopped planning and thinking, that everything made sense to me. I was sitting in the car next to my little brother, who has autism . . . [and] everything suddenly made sense. Speech therapy, where I can help people like my brother whose intelligence is underestimated due to his autism, suddenly became my purpose. . . . The beauty of it all was that it came to me when I was doing absolutely nothing.

Shayna Heichman, "When You Still Don't Know What to Do with Your Life," *Tiny Buddha* (blog), 2018. https://tinybuddha.com.

no real level of commitment in any of them. According to Daniel L. Schwarz, who teaches English literature at Cornell University, "Selective colleges favor for admittance those who play a leadership role in such activities, in part because such activities at a more advanced level play a vital role in college life and in part because the best advertisement for a college are alumni playing a leadership role in their communities and perhaps on the state and national level."[6]

Sticking with a Major Can Be Hard

Still another thing to think ahead about when considering attending college are personal interests. That is, what subjects and/ or activities most fascinate you or would you like to spend time studying? Carrying that one step further and couching it in terms of a possible future career, the ultimate question will be: What do you want to be when you grow up?

A great many colleges expect their applicants to be thinking about the future exactly that way. So they tend to require, or at least urge, applicants to declare a major—a principal area of study—from the outset. Indeed, some schools actually discourage students from changing majors later, saying that doing so adds too much extra time and cost to a person's education. Philadelphia's Chestnut Hill College is only one of several colleges that counsel students to stick with their initially chosen majors.

Yet a great many young college students *do* switch their majors at least once. According to the US Department of Education, at least a third of college freshmen and sophomores end up changing their majors, and 10 percent of college students in general switch majors two or more times. The reason for this is that

College students need solid reading, writing, research, and note-taking skills. High school students who plan to attend college should work to develop these skills.

many young people today have a wide range of interests, says Chestnut Hill's president, Carol Jean Vale. "Many more now than was true in the past," she says, "come [to this school] without being absolutely certain what they want to do. There are so many options open to them, so many things that they're interested in, that settling on one thing can be very difficult."[7]

And don't feel bad if, at the age of sixteen or eighteen, you don't know what you want to do for the rest of your life. You're not alone. Many of your peers are in the same boat—as are a lot of people who are even older than you.

Acquiring Basic Skills

No matter what one chooses for a major, arriving at college with certain basic academic skills is a huge plus. Indeed, studies have shown that many college freshmen lack such skills and as a result have a harder time adjusting to college life. Middle school and high school are the logical places to develop those skills, one of the most important of which is effective time management. To succeed in higher education, Schwarz explains,

> you need to develop time management and disciplined study habits as early as middle school. It is a good idea to keep track in writing or keep a computer file of how you are using your time. You need to set aside specific times for study and during those times you should turn off the TV and put the smart phone away. Realistically, you might begin with 30 to 40 minute study periods but by your later high school years you should be able to concentrate without a break for between 60 to 90 minutes.[8]

"You need to develop time management and disciplined study habits as early as middle school."[8]

—Cornell University English professor Daniel L. Schwarz

Solid reading and writing abilities are also important, as are good verbal communication, research, and note-taking skills.

Some middle school and high school courses include instruction in how to take good notes, a skill that makes nearly every subject easier to learn. Even if they don't, students who are thinking about college should take the initiative and acquire that skill on their own. A number of helpful online sites offer pointers, including the best kinds of notebooks to use, how to write down the material in outline form, and how to organize the notes after class. "Remember," Schwarz says, "you can always edit material if you write down too much, but you cannot recoup material that you have forgotten. If you miss class, borrowing another student's notes is essential."[9]

Dealing with Stress

At some point or another, the pressures of doing well in high school, planning for college, having a social life, and meeting commitments at home can become overwhelming. It is not unusual for teens to feel considerable stress in high school. This is supported by a 2019 Pew Research Center survey which found that 61 percent of teens are stressed out by pressure to get good grades. Moreover, about six in ten of the teens interviewed said they were planning to attend college and that fact had increased the pressures they felt to do better academically.

Stress is a normal part of everyday life, but too much stress is not a good thing. So it's important for teens to find ways to create balance in their lives. Maddie Pfeifer wrote about her own attempt to strike that balance while attending La Salle Catholic College Preparatory, a high school in Milwaukie, Oregon:

> I can say that the college application process is unlike anything I have ever done before—it is much more time consuming, stressful, and at times confusing, than I would have ever thought. Up until the day I applied, my house was often filled with yelling, arguments, and tears as the stress affected not only me, but my parents too. As I talked to my friends about the stress I was experiencing, I found

Improving Your Reading and Writing Skills

Reading and writing skills are paramount for a successful college student, says Cornell University English professor Daniel L. Schwarz. He gives the following advice to high school students planning for college:

> The best preparation is to learn how to read carefully and thoroughly whether it be fiction or non-fiction. . . . Select your reading with discrimination and rely on suggestions from teachers and other well-read adults. It is important that you keep up with national and international news and issues and that you develop an interest in the world in which you live, including the rapidly changing world of science. Reading the *New York Times,* the best news source in the U.S., for a half hour daily will help.
>
> Reading well means reading skeptically and learning to find places in newspapers or online when arguments are not logical or require more imagination. Developing a critical intelligence is a crucial component of learning.
>
> Equally important to reading intelligently is developing your writing skills. That means taking every writing assignment seriously. It means learning to write drafts, and that requires beginning assignments as soon as they are given. Term papers can teach you how to do research and use the library and internet as research tools.

Daniel L. Schwarz, "How to Prepare for College," HuffPost, November 7, 2014. www.huff post.com.

out that I was definitely not alone, as they felt the same unbearable anxiety as me. . . . What I have learned throughout this stressful time is to . . . be as organized as possible in every way that you can, and despite how difficult it is to do, try not to stress so much.[10]

CHAPTER TWO

Finding the Right Fit

Aneesa Shaikh, who grew up in a suburb of Seattle, Washington, began working as a professional graphic artist in 2019. Today she still thinks about the career that almost didn't happen. The reason dates back to a decision she made in 2015 when she was still a high school senior. Like many of her peers at the time, she was struggling with which college to attend. When she finally made her decision, it turned out that the college she picked was not the right one for her. The school was more than 3,000 miles (4,828 km) from home and family and was located in a tiny rural community. From the start, she felt lonely and homesick being so far from family and friends. And the tiny community, so different from the large and vibrant city where she had spent her childhood, was another mismatch.

For those first few months of her college career, Aneesa was miserable. "I was supposed to be happy and excited like everyone else," she says.

So why couldn't I shake the feeling of complete isolation even in the presence of my roommates and other people? I thought things would get better once classes started, but sure enough, the more people I met, the more I got to know the school, and the deeper into the semester we got, the worse I felt. I hated the way I felt around my peers. I hated the culture/"vibe" of the campus when I was on campus for more than a day and a half. I hated the tiny town. I hated the size of the school . . . the campus felt claustrophobic.[11]

Live and Learn

Each year many thousands of high school seniors across the country make the same mistake that Shaikh did. The good news is that it's not a fatal mistake. Although the experience of choosing the wrong college can be really stressful and disappointing, most students recover fairly quickly by transferring to a different school that is a much better fit. They then chalk up the experience to the old "live and learn" adage. "The bottom line," Shaikh asserts, "is

Students walk through campus at the University of California, Berkeley. Public universities and colleges are partially subsidized by state governments, making tuition lower than at private schools.

Taking the Plunge into Community College

"I did not want to go to community college," aspiring makeup artist Daniela Romero writes in the online magazine *Affinity*. In fact, she recalls, attending community college had never entered her mind until her mother "dropped the news on me junior year of high school that there simply was not enough money to send me to a four-year college." Daniela was initially upset. Her impressions of community colleges were all pretty negative. "I believed what society wanted me to believe: that everyone who went to community college was only there because they couldn't get in anywhere else, that the classes at community college were easier and therefore, I wasn't being challenged as much as other college students were." But as time went on, she continues, she learned that attaining success in college has more to do with how hard a student works than with the type of college he or she attends. "In reality," she says, "professors and classes at community colleges are just as challenging and insightful" as those at most four-year colleges. "I strongly advise anyone who is considering community college to take the plunge."

Daniela Romero, "Why I Recommend Going to Community College," *Affinity*, January 6, 2018. http://affinitymagazine.us.

that leaving the school, coming back home, and starting again at a new place was one of the best things I've ever done for myself. It enabled me to reflect on my experiences and process them in a meaningful way that yielded a lot of important life lessons and new knowledge about myself, which I am very grateful for."[12]

One way to avoid picking a college that turns out to be the wrong fit is to do plenty of research on all of the schools you *think* you want to apply to. In addition, high school guidance counselors say, it is best to take plenty of time to mull over and weigh the various choices. In retrospect, Shaikh admits that she was too hasty in making her choice. The college in question has a glowing reputation, she points out, and is known to be unusually hard to get into. So when it accepted her, she felt as if she had accomplished something important and interpreted it as a sign that she was meant to attend that school. With a bit more thoughtful reflection, she adds, she might have made a more appropriate choice.

Different Approaches to Higher Learning

Certainly part of what can at times make choosing the right college difficult is that there are many different approaches to higher learning to pick from. Four-year colleges and universities—some public, others private—are plentiful. Public ones are typically state schools, such as the University of Missouri. Because they are partially subsidized by state governments, their tuition is usually lower and therefore more affordable than private schools. More affordability also means that such schools tend to have fairly large student bodies. The University of Missouri had thirty thousand students enrolled for 2019. Some public universities are even larger than that. In contrast, private colleges and universities, which come in all sizes, are partly funded by private donations and tend to have higher tuitions. Harvard University in Massachusetts is a well-known private university; its student population in 2018 was 36,000. Macalester College in St. Paul, Minnesota, is also private; its student body in 2018 numbered 2,174.

Still another approach is to attend a community college. These public colleges, which usually offer two-year degrees and certificate programs of various lengths, appeal to students who are looking for schools that are both local and affordable. Although they lack the reputations of most four-year schools, it is possible to get a good education at a community college. As the popular online educational site Education Corner reports, "Community college used to have a reputation of being less academically serious than traditional

> "Academic standards [for community colleges] have risen, as have the qualifications of the teachers."[13]
>
> —The online educational site Education Corner

four-year universities. But a lot has changed in the world of community college. Most importantly, academic standards have risen, as have the qualifications of the teachers."[13]

Indeed, a Columbia University research study conducted from 2005 to 2018 found that two years of study at most community colleges is roughly equal in quality to the first two years of study at most four-year schools. Many community college students begin

How Reliable Are College Rankings?

A lot of students (and their parents) are strongly influenced by national rankings when picking colleges. A number of entities issue such rankings each year. Among the most well known are *U.S. News & World Report*, the Princeton Review, and *Barron's*. But how important are these rankings when picking a school?

A 2018 survey by the Stanford Graduate School of Education explored this question. It compared the findings of several major academic studies conducted from 2012 to 2017 that examined whether the college rankings are an effective, reliable way to select a college. These studies, the Stanford survey stated, found no significant relationship between a college's high ranking and how much students actually learn at a school and how well they do professionally after college. The researchers state:

> Regardless of whether a student attends a college ranked in the top 5% or one ranked much lower, the research strongly suggests that engagement in college, how a student spends his or her time, matters much more in the long run than the college a student attends. . . .
>
> Instead, [students should] seek a good fit, a school where [they] can engage and participate fully in academic and social life in order to thrive both during the college years and beyond.

Stanford Graduate School of Education, "A 'Fit' over Rankings: Why College Engagement Matters More than Selectivity," 2018. https://ed.stanford.edu.

their postsecondary studies with the goal of transferring to a four-year college, where they will earn a bachelor's degree (or higher).

Match Academic Offerings with Academic Interests

Once a college-bound high schooler decides on the kind of college he or she wants to attend, there are a number of other more specific factors that can help inform the decision. Perhaps first and foremost is the matter of academic fit—that is, whether the academic programs a school offers match a student's interests and goals. The nonprofit educational and scholarship program Quest Bridge advises, "Whether or not you've decided what to study, it's important to attend a college that suits your general range of potential interests, your personality, and even your relative academic strength. When looking at colleges, ask yourself: Does the school have programs that fit my current and/or potential academic interests?"[14] So, for instance, if you're thinking about becoming an engineer, look for schools that have respected engineering programs. Or if you plan to pursue a career in public administration or teaching, for example, learn which schools have strong programs in those areas.

> **"Ask yourself: Does the school have programs that fit my current and/or potential academic interests?"[14]**
>
> The educational and scholarship program Quest Bridge

Student-teacher ratio is another factor worth considering. If possible, you might want to find out how many students the average professor at a particular college has in his or her classes. As is true of high school classes as well, the fewer students a teacher has, the more time he or she can devote to individual students.

Moreover, it's worth knowing whether professors at the school actually teach all their classes. Often at elite universities, professors who are renowned in their fields spend much of their time doing research and assign graduate students to run some or most of their undergraduate classes. If you would rather interact with all your professors in each and every class, a university of that type may not be a good fit for you.

Social Fit

The size of a college can also be an important factor for prospective students. Some prefer a larger school because they feel there will be more courses to choose from, more diversity, and/or a wider range of potential new friends to meet. One of the reasons Cady Cohen chose the University of Central Florida is its size. With about sixty-four thousand students, she was looking forward to being part of a diverse student population. She recalls:

> When I first arrived onto campus, I went into culture shock. I couldn't believe how large my school actually was and how small it made me feel. The initial awe took some time to wear off, but once it did, I knew I made the right decision. . . .
>
> The best part about attending a larger university is the amount of diversity you will encounter throughout the campus and community. In fact, if you attend a large enough university, you will meet tons of people from around the world. . . .
>
> You can make friends in the coffee shop, the student union, tailgating at football games, in your classes—it's effortless when you attend a large school.[15]

In contrast, some college-bound young people seek out a smaller school because they prefer a quieter, more intimate setting in which they can eventually be on a first-name basis with just about everyone on campus.

The social scene on and near campus can also be a consideration in choosing a college. For example, some high school students are eager to join a fraternity or sorority during their college career. If that's something that matters to you, make sure the colleges you apply to actually have fraternities or sororities.

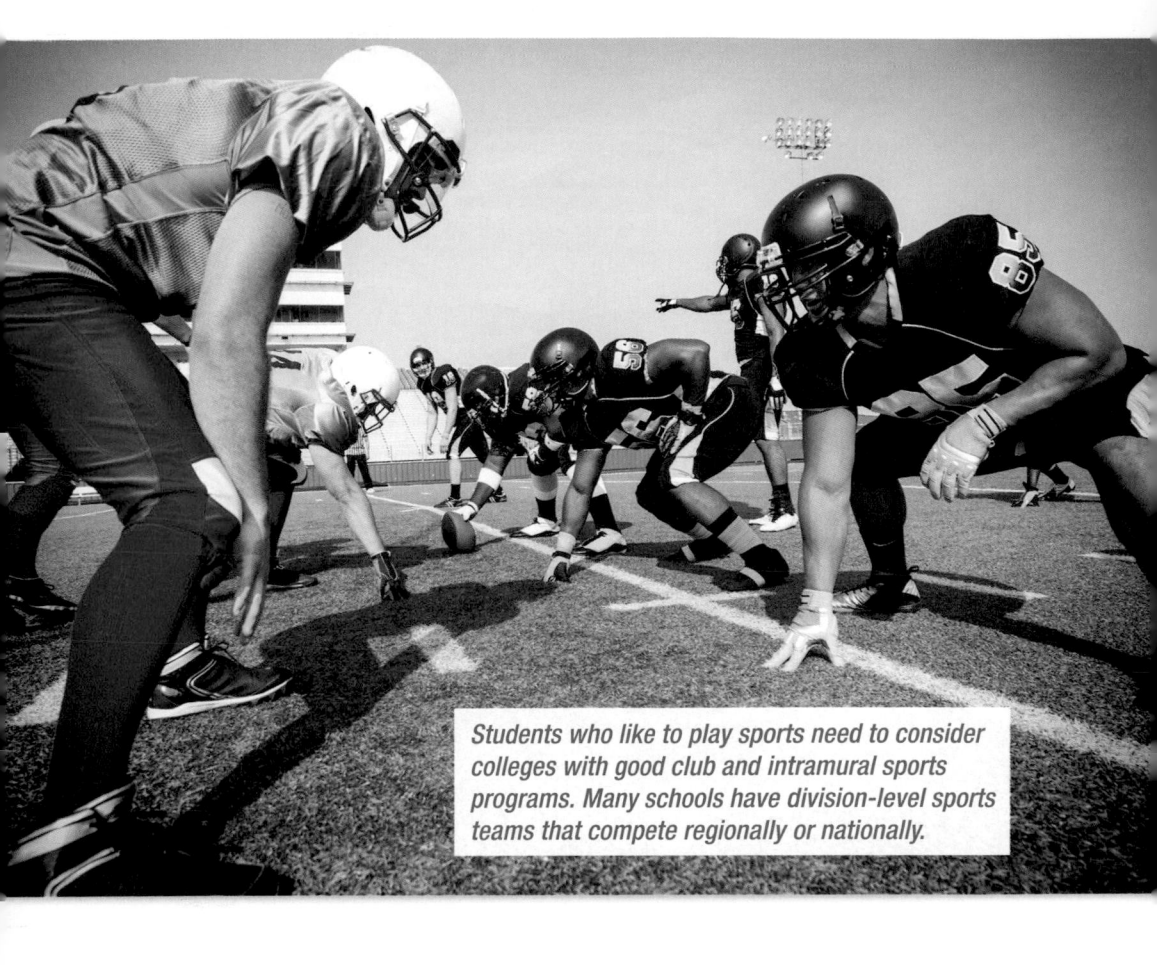

Students who like to play sports need to consider colleges with good club and intramural sports programs. Many schools have division-level sports teams that compete regionally or nationally.

Sports teams can be another deal maker or deal breaker. If your social life in high school revolved around Friday night football, weekly soccer matches, or swim meets and you want that to continue, you'll need to look for a college that has those kinds of programs. That definitely applies to athletes but also to fans. Most schools have club or intramural sports. Many, but not all, have division-level sports teams that compete regionally or nationally.

Initial Research into Potential Colleges

The usual advice given by high school counselors and other experts is to carefully look into academic programs, the social scene, and other features of college life even before deciding where to apply. This is good advice. The question is: Where do you begin? In the initial stages of the college search, college fairs and the Internet are probably two of your best information resources. Most high schools or school districts sponsor college fairs. These events usually feature representatives from dozens of colleges and universities, which is what makes college fairs a helpful way to investigate several schools in a brief time span. The representatives should be able to answer questions and provide brochures and other information about their respective institutions. To get the most out of these events, students should come with a list of specific questions. These can be questions about academic programs or extracurricular activities or even about school population or the surrounding community.

Although college fairs will be helpful to some students, online research is something all college-minded students can and should do. Many websites offer detailed information about colleges around the country (and abroad), including comparisons and critiques. Even more valuable are the personalized websites that all colleges now maintain, in large part as a way to reach out to and interest prospective students from far and wide.

Typical is the well-constructed website for Boston University in Massachusetts. It displays all manner of useful information, including the school's financial aid programs, research facilities, sports teams and gyms, and art-related and other extracurricular activities. Particularly helpful are the school's virtual tours—videos that take online visitors to student residential facilities, classrooms and science labs, and clubs and other social hangouts.

Another virtual tour introduces visitors to the many off-campus sites and activities available in the surrounding city. These include Boston's world-famous Museum of Science, the scenic Esplanade along the Charles River where music concerts are held, and historic Faneuil Hall and other surviving remnants of colonial America. Similar virtual tours offered by other colleges advertise their own local attractions in hopes of persuading high school students from around the nation to apply and join their next freshman class.

Letters of Recommendation

While planning ahead for which colleges to eventually apply to, high school juniors and seniors should also get a jump on acquiring letters of recommendation from teachers and counselors. Some schools no longer require them, while others ask for several. College-bound students should check a prospective college's website to see whether it requires such letters, and if so, how many. The rationale used by the schools that *do* require them is that young candidates for college are part of an extremely large pool of applicants from all parts of the country. Such letters can help you stand out from many others in that pool. For example, teacher recommendations constitute concrete examples of your abilities in a subject area; a recommendation from a guidance counselor, meanwhile, can show college officials where you stand academically among your classmates.

Thus, whether you are picking out the colleges that will be the best fit, taking virtual tours of those schools, or collecting letters of recommendation, as a college-bound high schooler you need to do your homework. In the words of the useful online college admissions advice website CollegeVine, you should do your best to show colleges "the qualities that make you an interesting and unique human being and a great addition to a college campus."[16]

CHAPTER THREE

Campus Tours

In the spring of 2018 Edward, a high school senior in Falmouth, Massachusetts, visited the campus of Syracuse University in upstate New York. He took the general campus tour offered by the school, which introduced him to the main points of interest on the sprawling campus. They included some typical classrooms, the 49,250-seat Carrier Dome football stadium, and one of the school's several dorms. But what most interested the young man was the university's nationally famous drama department. He recalls:

> I caught the acting bug in high school. So I decided to major in theater in college, and Syracuse was one of the nine schools I was looking at that had good reputations for drama. Syracuse especially interested me because it has Syracuse Stage, a professional theater company that works closely with the university's drama students. I spent hours there and asked what seemed like hundreds of questions.[17]

As it turned out, Edward did not end up attending Syracuse. He decided to go with one of the other colleges he applied to. In all, he applied to nine schools but visited only two of them. It's not uncommon for students to apply to that many schools. It's also not uncommon for kids to not visit all of the schools they apply to. Given the cost and time involved, that's just too many schools for most people to be able to visit. "Depending on how close to home a college is," *Forbes* magazine contributor Troy Onink writes, "the expense of visiting can climb into the thousands of dollars when you start adding air fare, car rentals, hotel rooms, and meals for parents, the student, and often siblings too."[18]

Thus, most college-bound students who apply to multiple schools manage to visit only a fraction of the campuses in person. Usually they rely on online virtual tours to investigate the rest. As might be expected, surveys show that the vast majority of the final choices are schools the students did take the time and effort to visit in the flesh.

Benefits of In-Person Visits

College admissions officials say that physical campus tours are superior to virtual ones for several reasons. First, they point out, a five- or ten-minute video of a campus, no matter how expertly produced, cannot duplicate the experience of actually exploring that campus in person for several hours or more. In the words of a spokesperson for the admissions office at Flashpoint Chicago, a campus of Columbia College Hollywood, in downtown Chicago that trains young filmmakers:

> You've probably spent a good amount of time on college websites looking at photos and videos, but seeing a campus for yourself is an entirely different experience. You'll get to walk through the actual classrooms you'll be learning in, see some of the equipment you'll be working with, and experience the overall "feel" of the campus. From dining halls to dormitories, you will have a chance to see it all.[19]

Another advantage is that, although a student or school official will guide you around the campus, after the formal tour is over you can go back and spend more time in selected locations that caught your interest earlier. Also, during the trip the visitor is not confined to the campus itself. He or she can, and in fact is strongly advised to, explore the town or city in which the college is situated. This is valuable because, as the Flashpoint Chicago spokesperson says, "college isn't all study all the time. Exploring the city surrounding the campus will give you the opportunity to see if this is a place you can really put down your roots."[20]

In addition, visiting a campus in person allows an interested high schooler to ask many questions, some planned and others spontaneous—something one cannot do in a virtual tour. The tour guide will be able to answer some of the questions. However, you will learn a lot more about the school and what it has to offer if you question several different people. Moreover, stopping random students and asking for their honest opinions can be highly illuminating. Edward recalls that while visiting Emerson College in Boston,

> my dad and I met a student outside a coffee house and she was nice enough to answer some personal questions, including what she thought about the quality of the pro-

Prospective students take a guided tour of UCLA. College admissions officials say that physical campus tours are better than virtual tours. No video clip can duplicate the real experience of exploring a campus in person.

EVELYN & MO
OSTIN MUSIC CENTER

College Students Recall Their Campus Tours

College Board, an organization that offers expert advice on preparing for college, asked several college students whether their campus tours had affected their choice of which school to attend. Tahlia responded:

> What helped me [choose] was to plan my own "adventure day" there, apart from the tour. After making a few phone calls, I was able to attend a couple of classes, talk to some professors and coaches, [and] spend a night in the dorms.

Bianca recalled:

> After visiting my dream school, I was highly disappointed. Something about the atmosphere and interacting with the students didn't satisfy me. But when I visited the college I'm at now, I felt an instant sense of comfort. I was able to speak with the diversity-enhancement representatives, and they were extremely nice and welcoming. I knew this was the campus I had to attend, and I do not regret my decision.

Gregory said:

> Looking online and through college catalogs helped me narrow down which institutions matched my academic needs, but I didn't realize that [my college] was the place I could call home until I stepped foot on campus and stayed overnight with a student.

College Board, "Students Speak: How Campus Visits Helped Me Choose," 2019. https://bigfuture.collegeboard.org.

fessors who teach the regular, non-theater courses. She said that some were better than others but that overall the teachers there are first-rate. She was very polite and open about everything and we really appreciated her input.[21]

Because Edward planned to major in theater, during the same tour he and his father also scheduled a meeting with a professor who teaches in the drama department. In a session lasting more than half an hour, the professor provided detailed information about how the department operates, the opportunities in acting and stagecraft for motivated students, and the expectations the professors have of those students. Edward felt the meeting was highly productive because much of what he learned in it was not available in the school's brochures or on its website.

When to Go

Figuring out when to do college visits requires some logistical planning. Colleges offer pertinent information on their websites. There are also general college-related online sites that have such information. One of the best is that of College Board, a nonprofit group that provides advice about all aspects of preparing for college. About campus tours, the site says it is "best to visit colleges before your applications are due. That way, you can be confident you would be happy at any of the colleges you're applying to."[22]

"[It is] best to visit colleges before your applications are due. That way, you can be confident you would be happy at any of the colleges you're applying to."[22]

—The college prep experts at College Board

While this might be ideal, it isn't practical for many students, especially if they are applying to multiple colleges and some or all of them are far from home. For this reason, other experts suggest making an effort to visit nearby colleges early in the process and waiting until after acceptance to visit more-distant campuses.

If you can manage it, visiting a college when school is in session is a good idea. That will give you the most realistic picture of the campus and its student body. The best months to visit are generally from September to early December (before winter break) and mid-January to March. But doing campus tours during those months might require you to take time off from school—which not every-

Can Campus Tours Be Misleading?

Although many experts on college admissions agree that campus tours can be useful in choosing which college to attend, some take a dimmer view of this approach. In an article for the *New York Times*, psychologist and educator Erica Reischer offers a perspective that suggests that campus tours, in and of themselves, can be misleading and not as useful as most people assume.

> It's challenging to imagine attending a college we haven't seen yet, so visiting the campus—to take a tour, meet students, get the lay of the land—seems like a prerequisite to making a good decision. But visiting a college is not the same as being a student there, and this distinction matters a lot, because of the many ways in which our imagination misleads us. As a decision-making tool, imagination is inherently flawed. It necessarily omits significant details, while filling in gaps and leaving out other features in such a way that we don't notice what we've made up or what is missing. . . . Whatever students see or experience during a brief campus visit—whether it's a sunny day or an ill-prepared tour guide—will inevitably stand out and have a disproportionate effect on their decision-making.

Erica Reischer, "Skipping the College Tour." *New York Times*, April 26, 2017. www.nytimes .com.

one can (or should) do. High schools in some states allow an excused absence to visit a prospective college. (You should check your own high school's policy on this before planning such a trip.)

Guided Tours

Experts also advise signing up ahead of time for whatever official tour the college in question offers. Exploring the campus and adjoining town on your own is worthwhile. But taking the official tour is a good way to get a full view of the various areas of the campus, guided (usually) by a student who can tell you what you're looking at and answer questions. Moreover, the official guide may be able to get you into buildings that are open only to the school's teachers and students.

A typical campus tour lasts about two hours, and colleges purposely structure these excursions to include as wide a range of campus attractions and helpful information as possible. The two-hour outing presented on weekdays at 10:00 a.m. and 1:30 p.m. by the University of Utah in Salt Lake City is a good example. As the school's website describes it, the tour "includes an admissions information session, a walking tour of our campus led by a University Ambassador [official student guide] who will share

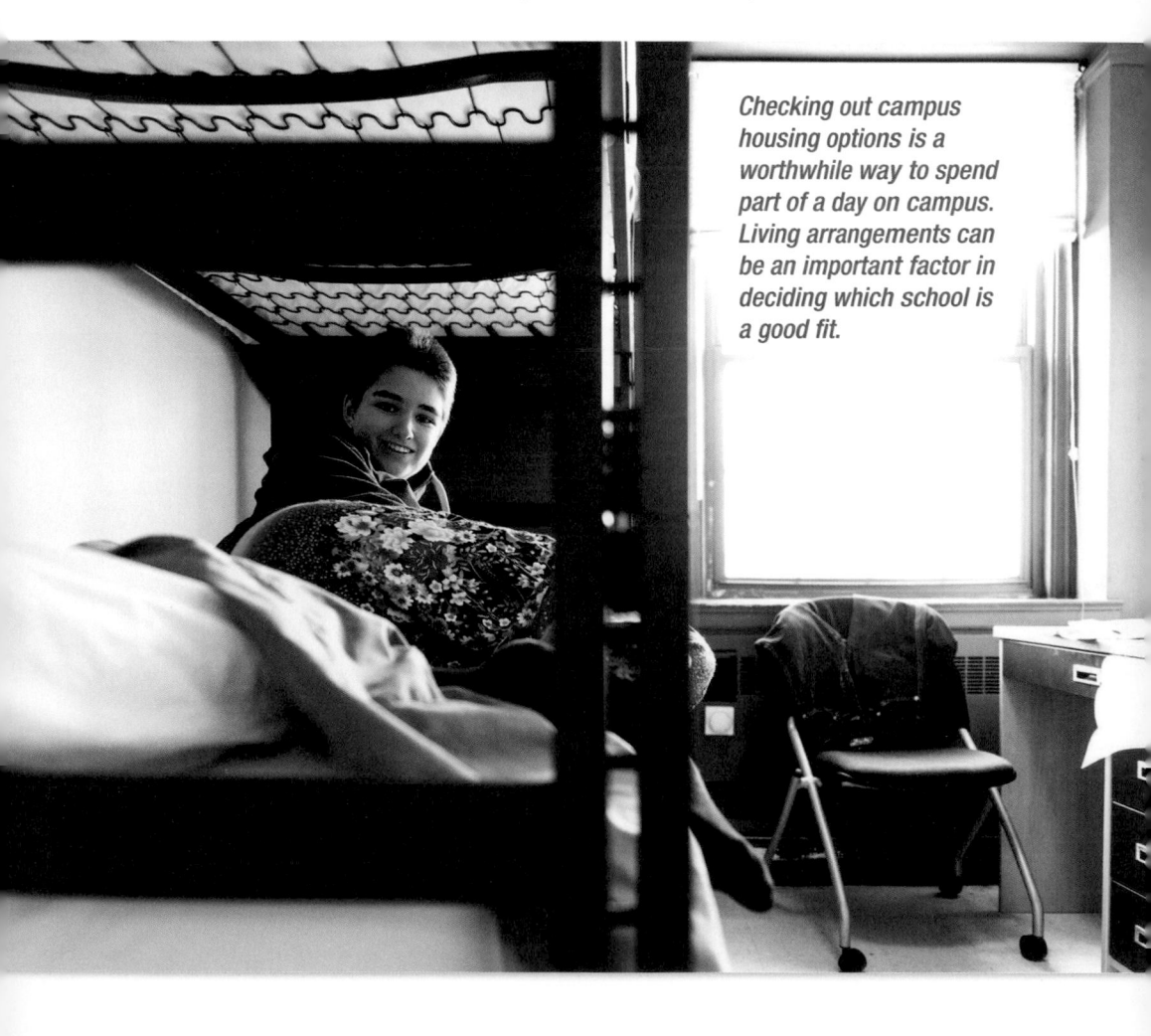

Checking out campus housing options is a worthwhile way to spend part of a day on campus. Living arrangements can be an important factor in deciding which school is a good fit.

with you some history and traditions, information about student life, getting involved, academics, and their unique student experience, and a preview of our housing facilities."[23]

Checking out housing and dining options is a worthwhile way to spend part of a day on campus. Either on or off the official tour, it's a good idea to visit the dorms and other campus housing options. Most dorms have shared rooms and bathrooms; some have more private rooms or suites. For some students, the distance from dorms to classrooms could be a factor. And where to eat is usually a concern for just about everyone. This would be a good time to check out the local food establishments, either on campus or nearby.

Listen to Your Gut

Doing a college tour gives you a more realistic picture of what life at that school and in that city or town will be like, but it doesn't guarantee you're going to like it once you start school there. Likewise, not doing an in-person campus tour doesn't mean that you won't like the place once you move in and classes begin. Campus tours are worthwhile if you can do them. But if you can't visit any of the colleges you're considering, don't stress about it. A school's website, brochures, and virtual tours *will* provide a rough idea of what getting an education there will be like. Campus tours are just another tool for helping you decide what school to attend. Some experts suggest that if visiting your preferred college is impossible, you should tour at a nearby campus, even if you know you will not be attending that school. This approach will at least provide a fairly realistic picture of life on a college campus.

If you *can* tour your preferred school or schools, make such visits as useful and memorable as possible. College Board advises, "Listen to your gut. Do you feel comfortable walking around campus? Do you feel at home? Do you click with the students and faculty? Is this what you imagined college to be like? Spending time on a campus helps you determine whether a college is a good fit."[24]

CHAPTER FOUR

Tests, Tests, and More Tests

Like many of her classmates, Florida high school senior Toni Velazquez felt anxious about the upcoming SAT. A standardized exam designed to measure students' readiness for college, it has been administered each year by College Board since 1926. Before the big test day, Velazquez did her best to prepare in practice sessions, especially for the twenty-five-minute section in which students have to produce a well-written essay. She thought she was reasonably well prepared, but she still found the time pressure to be a challenge. Velazquez says:

> Despite writing several practice essays, I didn't fully understand the impact of the 25-minute time limit until I actually wrote a real essay on test day. The time went by much faster than expected, and although I was able to finish in time with a four-paragraph essay, I had to pack in a conclusion at the last minute and barely had any time to edit the rest. [Practice] definitely helps with cutting down on time, but ultimately you only have 25 minutes to plan and write your essay, so it's basically a given that you're going to be forced to rush.[25]

The SAT and ACT Compared

Many US colleges and universities still employ a standardized test as one of several entrance requirements for new students. Some schools prefer the SAT, while others prefer the ACT. Most accept either one.

A few colleges and universities have actually abandoned the standardized test requirement entirely. By 2019, according to the National Center for Fair & Open Testing, or FairTest, more than eight hundred American colleges no longer required or considered those scores. These schools "recognize that neither the SATs nor ACTs measure what students most need to succeed in higher education," says FairTest representative Bob Schaeffer. "Even the tests' sponsors admit that an applicant's high school record remains a better predictor of college performance than either exam is."[26]

High school students who apply to colleges that still require the exams most often take them during their junior or senior year (and sometimes both). Whichever test they take, they must achieve a certain minimal score or above in order for a college that requires such tests to accept them. Although both exams are overall equivalent in several ways, there are some notable differences. The time limit of the main section of the SAT, which primarily tests aptitude in reading and math, is three hours (plus twenty-five minutes for the essay, which is optional). Students who do the SAT can also take one or more one-hour exams in twenty specific subject areas, among them world history, literature, biology, French, and Spanish. In contrast, the ACT consists of a single, more general exam that tests students on their knowledge of English, math, reading, and science. It has a three-and-a-half-hour time limit (plus another forty minutes for an optional essay).

"Despite writing several practice essays, I didn't fully understand the impact of the 25-minute time limit until I actually wrote a real essay on test day. The time went by much faster than expected."[25]

—Florida high school senior Toni Velazquez

A proctor monitors students as they take the SAT. Even with significant preparation, many students are still surprised by the difficulty of the exam. Some underestimate test time constraints and fail to finish portions of the test.

Deciding Which Exam to Take

Considering the similarities between the two tests—and the fact that most schools accept either one—at first glance it's hard to know which one to take. Yet in spite of the exams' similarities, veteran teacher Hannah Muniz explains, there are some differences that are worth noting. If a person hates feeling crunched for time when taking exams, for example, Muniz recommends the SAT over the ACT because the SAT provides slightly more time per question than the ACT does.

The two tests have other differences. Muniz points out that the ACT contains a section completely devoted to science, whereas the SAT does not. "Science constitutes one-fourth of your total

ACTs score," she says. "So if you're a science whiz who loves the idea of having an entire section focused on scientific data, graphs, and hypotheses, the ACTs may be a better fit for you."[27] Muniz describes another way the two tests differ. She says the SAT has a lot of questions that require test takers to identify specific passages within text that support their answers. These types of questions might work better for students who are good at evidence-support questions. The ACT, she says, does not have questions like this.

A College Decides to Drop Standardized Tests for Applicants

Hampshire College in Amherst, Massachusetts, eliminated the SAT and ACT from its application process in 2014. Hampshire president Jonathan Lash explains why his school made this decision:

> If we reduce education to the outcomes of a test, the only incentive for schools and students to innovate is in the form of improving test-taking and scores. . . . Our greatly accelerating world needs graduates who are trained to address tough situations with innovation [and] ingenuity. . . .
>
> SATs/ACTs are strongly biased against low-income students and students of color, at a time when diversity is critical to our mission. . . .
>
> Some good students are bad test takers, particularly under stress, such as when a test may grant or deny college entry. . . .
>
> [In place of those tests] we've developed much better, fairer ways to assess students who will thrive at our college. In our admissions, we review an applicant's whole academic and lived experience. We consider an applicant's ability to present themselves in essays and interviews, review their recommendations from mentors, and assess factors such as their community engagement.

Jonathan Lash, "Results of Removing Standardized Test Scores from College Admissions," Hampshire College, September 21, 2015. www.hampshire.edu.

A lot of high school students eliminate the need to choose between the exams by taking both of them. One reason to do this is to see whether a student does better on one or the other. If the student gets a better score on the ACT than the SAT, for instance, he or she might decide to take the ACT again in hopes of getting an even better result. But taking these tests more than once can be costly. The Princeton Review advises, "The best way to decide if taking the SATs, ACTs, or both tests is right for you is to take a timed full-length practice test of each type. Since the content and style of the SAT and ACT are very similar, factors like how you handle time pressure and what types of questions you find most challenging can help you determine which test is a better fit."[28]

> "The best way to decide if taking the SATs, ACTs, or both tests is right for you is to take a timed full-length practice test of each type. Since the content and style of the SAT and ACT are very similar, factors like how you handle time pressure and what types of questions you find most challenging can help you determine which test is a better fit."[28]
>
> —Princeton Review

The Princeton Review is only one of several reputable organizations that provide such practice exams online. These practice exams measure the same kind of general knowledge that the main sections of both the SATs and ACTs test for. Meanwhile, because the essays are optional in both exams, students always face the decision of whether to take the essay section. The smartest approach, the experts say, is for a student to check with the schools he or she plans to apply to and find out if they prefer to see the essays.

Test Prep: Is It Worth It?

With the emphasis placed on test scores by some colleges, educator James S. Murphy asks whether it is any wonder that students are anxious about taking these exams. "Prep companies step in to relieve that anxiety," he says, "in the same way that doctors treat illness."[29] Murphy's use of the words *prep companies*

Students study in a college test prep class. The college test prep industry—which includes workbooks, how-to videos, in-person and online courses, and private tutors—generated $5 billion in 2018.

is shorthand for the enormous test-preparation industry that exploded in the early 2000s in the United States and around the world. Among other things, it includes workbooks, how-to videos, in-person and online courses, and in-person and online private tutors. Test prep can cost as little as a few dollars for a workbook or can run into thousands of dollars for various classes and private tutoring. The industry as a whole took in more than $5 billion in 2018, and that figure is expected to keep growing well into the 2020s.

As for whether sinking all that money, time, and effort into prepping for the SAT and/or ACT is actually helpful and therefore worth it, opinions differ. One thing the test-prep courses do offer are strategies for dealing with timed tests and different types of questions. For instance, some urge students to first answer questions they're sure of and then, if there's time, to go back to the questions they didn't know. Most also include practice tests, which some students swear by—others not so much.

Standardized test scores are not the only factors that go into college admissions decisions. College representatives say that they place more emphasis on grades, extracurricular activities, and letters of recommendation (when these are required) than on test scores. William Hiss, the former dean of admissions for Bates College in Maine, believes that the principal indicator of how a student will perform in college is his or her grade point average, or GPA. The evidence, he asserts, "clearly shows that high school GPA matters. Four-year, long-term evidence of self-discipline, intellectual curiosity, and hard work; that's what matters the most."[30] If a student's high school grades are low, he says, yet that student scores high on the SAT or ACT, the grades are a more accurate predictor than the test scores.

The thing to remember is this: How you do on the SAT or ACT does matter (especially if you're applying to a college with

Math and the ACT

California-raised and educated teacher Hannah Muniz has closely studied the SAT and ACT and supplies a detailed analysis of the differences between the two tests in an online blog. One of the chief differences, she says, involves the importance that one exam places on math. "How big of a role will Math play in your final score?" she asks her readers.

The answer to this question depends on whether you're taking the ACT or SAT. On the ACT, Math accounts for one-fourth of your total score (your Math section score is averaged with your other three section scores). On the SAT, however, Math accounts for half of your total score, making it twice as important on the SAT!

So if math isn't your strong suit, consider opting for the ACT. With the ACT, a lower Math score won't negatively affect your total score as much as it will on the SAT.

Hannah Muniz, "ACT vs. SAT: 11 Key Differences to Help You Pick the Right Test," *Prep-Scholar* (blog), June 25, 2018. https://blog.prepscholar.com.

an impacted program—meaning one that has way more applicants than openings and therefore only accepts a limited number
of students each year). But GPA often matters more. Having a
strong GPA is one of the best ways to ensure that you get into the
college or university of your choice.

Rest Easy

Nevertheless, the fact that large numbers of colleges still look at
such exam scores means that millions of high school students will
continue to take the SATs and ACTs each year for the foreseeable
future. No doubt many of them will, as so many have done in the
past, undergo a lot of stress before and/or during the tests. Experts offer advice in ways to avoid that stress. "Don't freak out,"
says Kathryn Knight Randolph, an expert on trends in college admissions. Your GPA matters more to admission officers than your
test scores, she explains. "There's just no need to stress out too
much about a low test score if you're a good student with a great
GPA." Moreover, when future employers consider hiring you, they
will not care about your old test scores. "So rest easy," she adds.
"A bad SAT score isn't going to ruin your whole life."[31]

CHAPTER FIVE

How Do You Pay for College?

When he was a senior at a Massachusetts high school in 2018, Jack was worried about where he would find the money to attend college. Although he describes his family as lower middle class, he describes himself as a diligent student who received mostly high grades. Moreover, he argues passionately, his years of hard work in school should be the deciding factor in whether he could benefit from a college education. "A student's ability to go to college should be based upon their academic success, not on their family's financial status," he told a *New York Times* reporter who was surveying student reactions to rising college costs. Some students, Jack continued,

> might be discouraged from even considering college simply based on its affordability. Students who truly want to succeed deserve to experience college regardless of the cost. If a young adult actually wants to learn, they should be given the opportunity. A desire to learn new things is a sign of someone that can do great things in their future. If your family can't provide enough money, that shouldn't be the factor that decides your future for you.[32]

Skyrocketing College Costs

Jack's uneasiness about how to pay for college is not unusual. A 2019 Pew Research Center survey revealed that many students who plan to attend a four-year college are not sure whether they can afford it. College costs have grown in recent years. Those costs include a lot more than tuition. A typical college student must also pay for books, housing, food, and sometimes transportation.

Lumping all those separate costs into one overriding figure, the average price tag for a college education has seriously outpaced increases in workers' wages during the past half century. According to the American Association of University Women, since 1976 the cost of college attendance has skyrocketed at least 150 percent (at some schools 200+ percent), while average US household incomes rose only 20 percent in the same period. Those cost increases have been particularly rapid and steep for prestigious private colleges. A recent CNBC report on college costs points to the fact that "a 1988 graduate of Harvard University would have spent $17,000 on tuition during his senior year. Now in his 50s, he would have to pay $44,990 in tuition for his own child to attend Harvard today."[33]

Schools like Harvard are not the norm, but tuition costs for other colleges have also risen. CNBC's investigation revealed that in the 2017–2018 school year the average cost of tuition alone at US four-year public colleges was $9,970 per year. Meanwhile, the average tuition cost at four-year private colleges was $34,740 per year. These costs increased to $10,230 and $35,830 respectively in the 2018–2019 school year. The costs of housing, food, and so forth add thousands of dollars more to these figures.

> "If your family can't provide enough money, that shouldn't be the factor that decides your future for you."[32]
>
> —Jack, a Massachusetts high school senior in an interview with the *New York Times*

Family Income and Student Loans

A natural question that college-bound high school students and their parents ask is how they will manage to pay these costs.

College tuition increases have been particularly rapid and steep for prestigious private colleges, like Harvard University, pictured here.

Three of the principal avenues are family income and savings, scholarships and grants, and loans. A 2018 study by Sallie Mae, a well-known financial institution that offers thousands of student loans each year, found that in that year 47 percent of college costs came from family income and savings. Another 28 percent of those costs were covered by scholarships and grants awarded to college-bound students. The rest—about 25 percent—came from loans.

Only in a minority of cases does any one of these three avenues pay the entire cost of a student's higher education. More often two or all three of them combine to send someone to college. For example, a person's parents may come up with some of the money, and often the student will get a job to help pay for his or her own education. That same student may also acquire a modest scholarship.

When no scholarship is available and a student's family can't afford to foot the bill, however, that student will probably apply for a loan. By far the most common college educational loan program is the Federal Direct Loan Program. The major benefits for young borrowers are that the program offers low-interest loans, and in most cases the students don't have to have a strong credit history, as is the case when adults borrow money from banks and other sources. Also, the students have some generous leeway in paying back these federal loans. Typically, the first payment is not due until six months after the person graduates from college.

Federal student loans have helped a lot of kids go to college, but there is always risk in taking out a large loan. Loans do have to be repaid. Sometimes young people who have no experience with loans and debt don't have a realistic sense of the amount of money they're borrowing and will have to repay. Or they might

College Costs Too High?

In 2018 Caitlyn Pellerin, then a high school senior in Danvers, Massachusetts, was one of several young people across the country whom the *New York Times* interviewed in a study of rising student loan debts. Pellerin said in part:

> After high school, I will be attending college and hopefully veterinary school. If the average cost per year of a public college is $10,000, and I attend that college for the full four years, that is a total of $40,000. In addition, vet school can cost up to $250,000 for four years of education. Once I am completed with all eight years of undergraduate and veterinary schooling, I will have paid roughly $290,000 for my education. Personally, I find that the cost of college is unbelievable. It is unreasonable to expect to pay for college without being left in debt, unless you are one of the few lucky ones to be a millionaire. Colleges should be trying to decrease tuition costs in order to create equal opportunities for all students. I fear for the stress of scholarship applications, taking student loans, and being left thousands of dollars in debt as a twenty-something year old, due to furthering my education.

Quoted in *New York Times*, "What Students Are Saying About: College Tuition, Homework Help and Loneliness," October 18, 2018. www.nytimes.com.

hope to earn a certain amount of money right out of college, but that doesn't always happen. So when considering applying for a student loan, it's important to do some research, ask questions, and remember that a loan can be a useful option but can also become a burden.

Student loan debt has become a problem in recent years. According to a 2018 report in *USA Today*, those young adults who do take out loans for college leave school after four years with, on average, just over $39,000 of debt. Approximately 20 percent of the borrowers owe more than $100,000 at the end of their senior year. The stark reality is that debt from education loans is now higher in the United States than that from credit cards and car loans.

The potential consequences of those burgeoning student debts can be life altering. Unable to afford one's mortgage or rent, says Madison, a worried Georgia high school senior, "you might have to choose a different place to live." Also, "what you want to pursue in life—maybe working for a nonprofit organization—might be affected because [to keep paying the student loans] you have to provide more income than you can obtain working for so little."[34]

Community Colleges, Scholarships, and Grants

One way that more and more high school students are trying to avoid accumulating such enormous debt is to attend community college for the first two years and then transfer to a four-year college for the remaining two years. The average cost of attending a community college in 2019 was $4,835 per year, less than half the annual cost of a public four-year college. That, according to the Princeton Review, makes going to community college "an outstanding way to save money." It helps, the Princeton Review points out, that "there is a community college within commuting distance of 90 percent of the U.S. population, so convenience is a big selling point. If you have family obligations or just don't feel financially ready to strike out on your own, a community college can enable you to continue your education without breaking the bank."[35]

Whether attending community college or a four-year university, many students apply for scholarships or grants. Although those two terms are often employed interchangeably and both are forms of financial aid, they do differ slightly by definition. Grants tend to be need-based and are most frequently awarded to students from low-income families to supplement other sources of college money. The chief sources of college-related grants are the federal and state governments.

In contrast, scholarships are most often merit-based; that is, the recipients in a sense earn them by displaying unusual talent or meeting some other nonfinancial criteria. Each year the US Department of Education gives away about $30 billion of grant and scholarship money, and various private organizations and foundations provide many millions of dollars more. The most appealing part of getting grants and scholarships is that unlike loans, they do not have to be paid back. Scholarships often prove especially helpful to students entering small, private colleges. Many of those schools charge higher tuition than large public universities, yet private colleges also frequently offer generous scholarships.

> **"[Attending] a community college can enable you to continue your education without breaking the bank."[35]**
>
> —The Princeton Review, an organization that helps high school students prepare for college

A few scholarships—commonly awarded to students with excellent grades and/or major athletic talent—are large scale, ranging in the tens of thousands of dollars or more. They are frequently called "full-ride" scholarships. They generally pay for a person's tuition, books, room and board, and sometimes even transportation and other expenses.

Partial scholarships—ranging from a few hundred to a few thousand dollars—are far more common. Given by a school, educational foundation, community group, or wealthy individual, such a gift often (though not always) covers a single expense, such as books, housing, or a portion of the tuition. Good grades

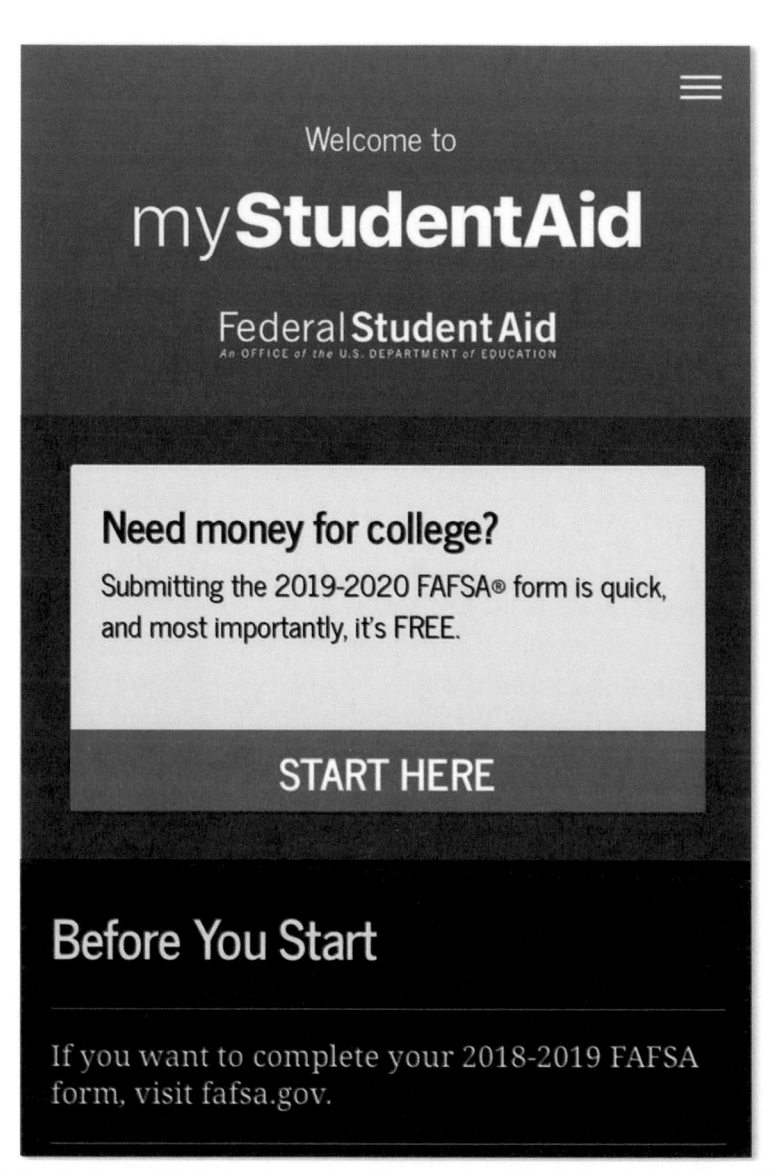

Applying for financial aid can be a daunting process. The federal government has tried to simplify that process by creating the Free Application for Federal Student Aid, or FAFSA for short. The phone app is pictured here.

and athletic ability may earn someone a partial scholarship. But many of these awards are given to students who excel in art, music, theater, and other extracurricular areas. Similarly, many private organizations sponsor scholarships for people from particular ethnic, cultural, or religious backgrounds.

A Financial Aid Clearinghouse

College Scholarships.org and Education Corner are only two of several reputable online sites that either list available scholarships and grants, explain how to apply for them, or both. In addition, information about these free sources of college money and about various kinds of student loans is available in the offices of virtually all high school guidance counselors. The websites of colleges and universities regularly list this sort of information as well.

Applying for financial aid for college can be a daunting process. The federal government has tried to simplify that process by creating the Free Application for Federal Student Aid, or FAFSA for short. It is a general form that students and their families fill out to apply for federal grants, loans, and work-study funds. FAFSA acts like a sort of financial aid clearinghouse because most colleges, state scholarship agencies, and foundations use it when deciding who will receive such aid.

College admissions officials and other experts on college preparation strongly urge all high school seniors to fill out the FAFSA form, even if they are not yet sure they need or want financial aid. First, most high schoolers and their families are eligible for some sort of grant, scholarship, or loan (or some combination of these). Any family that makes less than $250,000 per year can apply, and the vast majority of American families are in that financial range.

The experts also urge students to apply as early in a given school year as possible. This is because the government hands out the various kinds of aid on a first-come, first-served basis, and the sooner you apply the better your chances of receiving a grant, scholarship, or loan. Nicole Straub, who works for Discover Card's student loan program, points out that "October 1st is the day that the FAFSA form opens for the next academic period." She urges college-bound students to note that date and act fast. "We really encourage not only that all families fill out the FAFSA," she says, "but that they do so right away."[36]

The FAFSA form and the billions of dollars the government gives or loans to students seeking higher education are part of the

Originality in Scholarship Applications

In its helpful guide to applying for college scholarships and grants, the popular education website Education Corner urges students to be original and try to make their applications stand out from those of the many other students applying.

> Imagine that you're asked to review a thousand scholarship applications and to determine which applicant should receive a scholarship award. After reviewing all one thousand scholarship applications, you're about ready to keel over from exhaustion and boredom. All one thousand applications are really good [and] followed the application guidelines perfectly. But they were all pretty much carbon copies of one another. None of the applicants stood out from one another as original or unique. When preparing your scholarship application, it's important you follow all application rules and submission guidelines. This does not however mean you shouldn't be original. Remember, scholarship judges are people just like you and me. The last thing they want to do is review one thousand scholarship applications that are essentially the same. As you prepare your scholarship application, include information and exhibits that will help set you apart as interesting, unique and especially deserving.

Becton Loveless, "Guide on College and University Scholarships and Grants," Education Corner, 2019. www.educationcorner.com.

country's enormous educational network. This includes the colleges themselves, their admissions and financial officers, and all the institutions and private individuals who help students attend those schools. According to a US Department of Education spokesperson, all those institutions and individuals should work together to keep college costs reasonable. "Every hard-working student," the spokesperson says, "deserves a real opportunity to earn an affordable, high-quality degree or credential that offers a clear path to civic engagement, economic security, and success."[37]

CHAPTER SIX

Time to Apply

After all the preliminary prep work—researching colleges and universities online or at college fairs, taking the SAT or ACT, going on in-person or virtual campus tours, and learning about various funding sources—the college-bound student is finally ready to fill out applications. The vast majority of these forms are done online. So when the student clicks "send," all of his or her information reaches college admissions offices in a fraction of a second.

The time it takes to fill out a college application varies considerably from student to student. Some have more personal data, extracurricular activities, and so forth than others, which requires more time to describe. But experts say that at the very least you should be prepared to spend from several hours to a full day on a typical application.

One applicant who had more to report on his application than most others was a California native named Allen Cheng. He spent the better part of three days filling out his forms. In 2018 he posted his entire application online as a helpful guide to others and explained each step in detail. In addition to several extracurricular activities, he listed some academic honors he had received, fully realizing that all colleges are impressed by that sort of achievement. He recalls:

By far, the biggest academic honor I had was competing in the US National Chemistry Olympiad, where I ranked number 6 in the country in junior year, out of roughly 11,000 students. . . . If you are nationally or internationally ranked for something meaningful, you really stand out in the reader's mind, because most applicants only have regional and state honors, if even that. This . . . makes you stand out clearly from a bin of well-rounded applicants.[38]

The Common Application

Clearly, as Cheng's experience shows, filling out college applications can be a very time-consuming process. In part this is because most students apply to a *lot* of schools. Six or more is pretty typical. Eight to ten isn't uncommon. To shorten the application process, most students use the Common Application, or Common App. This online form enables students to fill out and submit just one application for most or all of the schools they are applying to. More than eight hundred US colleges and universities accept this online application. Other such platforms, each accepted by fewer schools than the Common App, include the Coalition App and the Universal App.

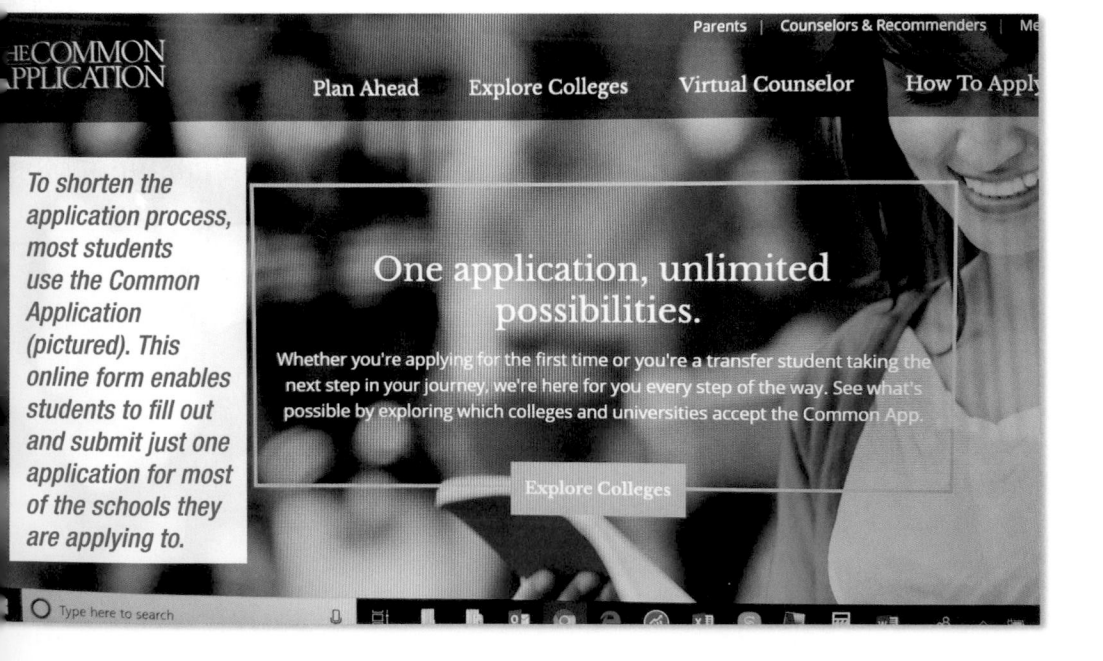

To shorten the application process, most students use the Common Application (pictured). This online form enables students to fill out and submit just one application for most of the schools they are applying to.

Lying on an Application

College admissions officials sometimes encounter real-life situations in which the actions of a few applicants stand out starkly against the backdrop of the hundreds of thousands of young people who apply to college each year. Sometimes, such individuals are remembered fondly for doing admirable things. But on occasion the opposite is true. Sally Goebel, a former admissions official at the Wharton School of the University of Pennsylvania, recalls a case in which an applicant used unethical means to get into the school. The young man in question submitted a moving essay about his mother's death, Goebel says, and that clinched his acceptance to Wharton. However, shortly before school started, someone in the admissions office needed the answer to a routine question and called the student's home. A woman answered the phone, and it quickly became clear that she was none other than the mother, who was very much alive. "It was kismet [fate]," Goebel asserts, still upset by the incident even after the passage of several years. "There wasn't any strategy there, and we didn't suspect him." Shocked school officials immediately withdrew the young man's admission, she remembers. Lying one's way into school is usually not worth it in the end, Goebel adds.

Quoted in Anemona Hartocollis, "'They're Not Fact-Checking': How Lies on College Applications Can Slip Through the Net," *New York Times*, December 16, 2018. www.nytimes.com.

Although applying online and using the Common App for multiple submissions definitely saves time and effort, these shortcuts have a notable drawback. Experts point out that filling out college applications in this manner can sometimes cause applicants to rush though the process. And rushing almost always results in making mistakes. One strategy to avoid such errors is to begin the process by printing out a hard copy of the blank application form. The student can then use the hard copy as a practice version of the application. Doing it by hand first, he or she can cross out words and scribble in corrections where necessary and later type the edited copy—hopefully devoid of errors—into the blanks in the on-screen version.

Gathering the Materials and Following Directions

Another benefit of printing out a blank hard copy of the application is that it reinforces with the applicant the various types of information the college wants on the form. That way, students can make a checklist of everything they'll need. With only occasional exceptions, college applications typically require information that falls into a series of traditional categories. These include the applicant's personal data (address, phone number, and other contact information); the courses taken in high school, especially in the junior and senior years; the grades the student received in those courses; a list of extracurricular activities; special academic honors earned, if any; scores from the SAT or ACT; letters of recommendation; and information about scholarships, FAFSA forms, and/or other financial data.

In addition, many colleges require students to include in the application an original essay—generally consisting of a few hundred words. If so, students should write a rough draft of the essay beforehand. Experts recommend polishing and proofreading the essay several times—either by hand or in a separate file—to produce a final version worthy of submission.

Once all these diverse materials have been collected and the student begins plugging them into the application, it is critical to follow the directions carefully. Not doing so is sure to cause mistakes, experts say, and college admissions officials have little patience with such errors. Some errors can actually result in the applicant being denied consideration. Each

> "[Our application has a place] marked clearly for international students. But we have gotten applications from American students who have not read that."[39]
>
> —Robert Barkley, an admissions official at Clemson University in South Carolina

year, admissions officials are inundated with applications containing careless mistakes. Robert Barkley, director of undergraduate admissions at Clemson University in South Carolina, recalls some common examples:

> We have a place on our application that is marked clearly for international students. But we have gotten applications from American students who have not read that, and where it asks, "Do you have a visa?" they say yes. And when it asks what kind, we're expecting to see [a foreign student visa]. In one case we got Bank of America. And where we asked for the number of the visa, we got the credit card number. We were not impressed.[39]

When the entire application has been completed to your satisfaction and you have proofed it several times for errors, it is finally time to take the plunge and click "send." Before you do, however, you should make sure to print out a hard copy of the finished forms for your own records. Or at the very least, copy the entire application and all additional documents to a flash drive. That way, if something unexpected happens, you'll have a copy to fall back on.

When to Apply?

Physically filling out and submitting the forms is not the only important aspect of the college application process. Students must also know *when* to submit their applications. Following a tradition recognized by the vast majority of colleges, a student applying for the fall semester of what will be his or her freshman year must meet an application deadline in late December or early January. Usually the applicant will hear back from the college or colleges on or about April 1.

If this is the route you choose, you must make sure to meet the deadline, since most colleges either ignore or discard late entries—even those that are only a few days late. A Texas high school senior named Brett Ferdinand, for example, was looking forward to attending the University of Texas at Austin. But he submitted his application late. He later recalled receiving a letter from the school "informing me that since my complete application had not been received by the deadline, I could not be admitted into the fall semester. This was not the response I had been hoping for."[40]

Applicants *can* choose other application routes, however, which might eliminate the dilemma Ferdinand found himself in. The most common of these alternate approaches is early decision, routinely called ED for short. ED is an option in which prospective students are allowed to apply in early to mid-November. There is both good news and bad news regarding ED. The good news is that an applicant will receive a decision by the college, one way or another, by mid- to late November. The bad news is that receiving a positive response eliminates the applicant's other

Schools communicate with applicants in different ways. Some colleges routinely get back to prospective freshmen through email, while others still notify applicants with traditional acceptance letters sent through the mail.

choices. As *U.S. News & World Report* contributing reporter Jordan Friedman points out, "If admitted under ED, applicants must enroll at that institution, with few exceptions, and withdraw any submitted applications to other colleges. Applicants may only apply ED to one school, experts say, so that university should be their first choice."[41]

Getting Accepted

Whichever approach applicants end up using, they most often receive word from the school or schools involved by late spring. (If the college uses rolling admissions, in which it processes applications as they are received, it might be early summer or even midsummer before the applicant hears back.) Schools tend to notify applicants in different ways. Some colleges routinely get back to prospective freshmen through email; others still notify applicants with traditional letters sent via snail mail; still others give applicants the choice of one or the other method.

If you hear from a college you want to attend and have been accepted, besides celebrating with family and friends, the first order of business is to lock in that school. This is most often accomplished by sending the admissions office a financial deposit that guarantees you a place in the upcoming freshman class. With rare exceptions, such deposits range from $50 to $500.

Some applicants luck out and are accepted by multiple colleges—in some cases *all* the schools they applied to. When that happens and the student remains unsure of which college to pick, talking to parents, high school counselors and teachers, or other trusted adults may help him or her weigh the choices. Also, this is a good time either to visit campuses you have not yet seen or to revisit one or two that you *have* seen.

Still another common scenario is when an applicant is accepted by one or more colleges but *not* by the one he or she most wanted to attend. Independent college counselor Jessica Velasco acknowledges that this situation is disappointing and frustrating. Yet, she cautions, all is not lost when a "denial letter comes from your 'dream school.'" It is only one of some common setbacks that many people have managed to overcome. In fact, she says, a fair number of highly successful people were rejected by their first-choice colleges. "Steven Spielberg was rejected from the University of Southern California (USC) School of Cinema Arts," she recalls. "He ultimately attended California State University, Long Beach and went on to win over 100 awards, including three Oscars."[42] Other successful individuals who were rejected by their dream schools include billionaire Warren Buffett and TV news anchor Katie Couric.

Finally, what if *all* of your college applications are rejected? Experts advise young people in that situation to consider one of various options, all of which can lead to positive outcomes. You can check to see whether there's still time to apply to a local community college. Once you've completed your general education courses at a community college, you can apply to transfer to a four-year school. Or some students decide to take a gap year, which is a year off from school between high school and college. Gap years are common in Europe and are becoming more popular in the United States. Possible pursuits during that period could be doing volunteer work, learning a trade, or traveling and seeing the country or the world. The most important thing to remember, Velasco says, is that "a denial letter is not the end of the world. Instead, it is a detour on the way to your ultimate goal of a college degree. Detours are not always the route you wanted to take, but sometimes you'll find them to be a better way to get to your destination."[43]

Annie Sullivan, the author of *A Touch of Gold*, agrees and adds that she had her "heart dead set on attending Notre Dame." After being rejected, she cried. But she says that in time she "ended up going to Indiana University, and honestly, it was amazing. I ended up exactly where I needed to be with amazing friends and faculty who have continued to shape my life to this day."[44]

> "A denial letter is not the end of the world."[43]
>
> —Independent college counselor Jessica Velasco

SOURCE NOTES

Introduction: Why Go to College?

1. Simon Fraser (website), "Why I'm Glad I Went to College," January 3, 2017. https://realsimon.com.
2. Quoted in James Link, "Thinking of Skipping College? Here are 6 Stats to Change Your Mind," Cornerstone University, January 10, 2017. www.cornerstone.edu.
3. Hispanic Scholarship Fund, "Preparing for College," 2018. www.hsf.net.

Chapter One: Thinking Ahead

4. Quoted in Greg Daugherty, "Getting Into College Is Easier than Applicants Think," *U.S. News & World Report*, March 8, 2017. www.usnews.com.
5. Quoted in Jacoba Urist, "Is College Really Harder to Get Into than It Used to Be?," *Atlantic*, April 2014. www.theatlantic.com.
6. Daniel L. Schwarz, "How to Prepare for College," HuffPost, November 7, 2014. www.huffpost.com.
7. Quoted in Jon Marcus, "Switching Majors Is Adding Time and Tuition to the Already High Cost of College," *Hechinger Report*. https://hechingerreport.org.
8. Schwarz, "How to Prepare for College."
9. Schwarz, "How to Prepare for College."
10. Maddie Pfeifer, "College Application Process Amplifies Stress of Senior Year," La-Salle *Falconer*, November 16, 2016. https://lasallefalconer.com.

Chapter Two: Finding the Right Fit

11. Aneesa Shaikh, "I Chose the Wrong College," Student Voices, November 12, 2016. https://mystudentvoices.com.
12. Shaikh, "I Chose the Wrong College."
13. Education Corner, "Community Colleges vs. Universities," 2019. www.educationcorner.com.
14. Quest Bridge, "Applying for College: Choosing a College," 2016. www.questbridge.org.
15. Cady Cohen, "Too Big to Fail," Study Breaks, August 3, 2017. https://studybreaks.com.
16. Monikah Schuschu, "How Important Are Letters of Recommendation?," *Applying to College* (blog), CollegeVine, October 7, 2016. https://blog.collegevine.com.

Chapter Three: Campus Tours

17. Edward, interview by Don Nardo, Falmouth, MA, February 8, 2019.
18. Troy Onink, "New Study Highlights How College Visits Boost Admissions Chances at Selective Colleges," *Forbes*, August 23, 2017. www.forbes.com.
19. Flashpoint Chicago, "Three Reasons You Need to Visit College Campuses," 2018. https://flashpoint.columbiacollege.edu.
20. Flashpoint Chicago, "Three Reasons You Need to Visit College Campuses."
21. Edward, interview.
22. College Board, "When to Visit," 2019. https://bigfuture.collegeboard.org.

23. University of Utah Office of Admissions, "Take Campus Tour!," 2019. https://admissions.utah.edu.
24. College Board, "When to Visit."

Chapter Four: Tests, Tests, and More Tests

25. Toni Velazquez, "The First Time I Took the SAT," CollegeXpress, March 2, 2016. www.collegexpress.com.
26. Quoted in Huffington Post, "SAT, ACT No Longer Required for Admission to 800 U.S. Colleges and Universities," November 28, 2012. www.huffingtonpost.com.
27. Hannah Muniz, "ACT vs. SAT: 11 Key Differences to Help You Pick the Right Test," *PrepScholar* (blog), June 25, 2018. https://blog.prepscholar.com/act-vs-sat.
28. Princeton Review, "SAT vs. ACT: Which Test Is Right for You?," 2019. www.princetonreview.com.
29. James S. Murphy, "The SAT-Prep Industry Isn't Going Anywhere," *Atlantic*, March 2014. www.theatlantic.com.
30. Quoted in Sarah Sheffer, "Do ACT and SAT Scores Really Matter? New Study Says They Shouldn't," *PBS NewsHour*, February 19, 2014. www.pbs.org.
31. Kathryn Knight Randolph, "3 Reasons Not to Worry About the SATs," Fastweb, May 11, 2017. www.fastweb.com.

Chapter Five: How Do You Pay for College?

32. Quoted in *New York Times*, "What Students Are Saying About: College Tuition, Homework Help and Loneliness," October 18, 2018. www.nytimes.com.
33. CNBC, "Here's How Much More Expensive It Is for You to Go to College than It Was for Your Parents," November 29, 2017. www.cnbc.com.
34. Quoted in *New York Times*, "What Students Are Saying About."
35. Princeton Review, "4 Reasons to Consider Community College," 2019. www.princetonreview.com.
36. Quoted in Abigail Hess, "The FAFSA Is Now Open—Here's Why Every Student Should Fill It Out," CNBC, September 28, 2017. www.cnbc.com.
37. US Department of Education, "College Affordability and Completion: Ensuring a Pathway to Opportunity." www.ed.gov.

Chapter Six: Time to Apply

38. Allen Cheng, "My Successful Harvard Application," *PrepScholar* (blog), April 25, 2018. https://blog.prepscholar.com.
39. Quoted in Courtney Rubin, "Avoid These Big College Application Mistakes," *U.S. News & World Report*, September 11, 2013. www.usnews.com.
40. Brett Ferdinand, "A Missed Deadline Provides a Costly Lesson," *The Choice* (blog), *New York Times*, March 16, 2010. https://thechoice.blogs.nytimes.com.
41. Jordan Friedman, "Applying Early Decision: 10 Frequently Asked Questions," *U.S. News & World Report*, October 23, 2017. www.usnews.com.
42. Jessica Velasco, "Dealing with a College Rejection Letter: What It Means to Be Denied," College Raptor, March 24, 2019. www.collegeraptor.com.
43. Velasco, "Dealing with a College Rejection Letter."
44. Quoted in Bill Murphy Jr., "These 9 People All Got Rejected at Their First Choice Colleges. Here's How Their Lives Turned Out," *Inc.*, 2018. www.inc.com.

FOR MORE INFORMATION

Books

ACT, *The Official ACT Prep Guide*. New York: Wiley, 2018.

Lisa M. Arter, *College: The Ultimate Teen Guide*. Lanham, MD: Rowman and Littlefield, 2018.

James W. Lewis, *College Admissions: How to Get Into Your Dream School*. Charleston, SC: Amazon Digital Services, 2018.

Elaina Loveland, *Creative Colleges: Finding the Best Programs for Aspiring Actors, Artists, Designers, Dancers, Musicians, Writers, and More*. Naperville, IL: Sourcebooks, 2017.

Ethan Sawyer, *College Essay Essentials: A Step-by-Step Guide to Writing Successful College Admissions Essays*. Naperville, IL: Sourcebooks, 2016.

Internet Sources

CNBC, "Here's How Much More Expensive It Is for You to Go to College than It Was for Your Parents," November 29, 2017. www.cnbc.com.

Lela Moore, "5 Pearls of Wisdom About College for Students Starting Their First Year," *New York Times*, April 19, 2018. www.nytimes.com.

Farran Powell, "An Ultimate Guide to Understanding Financial Aid for College," *U.S. News & World Report*, July 3, 2018. www.usnews.com.

Quest Bridge, "Applying for College: Choosing a College," 2016. www.questbridge.org.

Steph Shyu, "Getting Rejected by My Dream College Was the Best and the Worst Thing to Happen to Me," Medium, December 19, 2017. https://medium.com.

Websites

CampusTours (www.campustours.com). This splendid website allows prospective college students to plug in the name of almost any college in the United States and hop immediately to informative videos of that school's campus.

College Board (www.collegeboard.org). College Board, the organization that runs the SAT, provides a wealth of information about colleges, how to apply to them, and practically all other aspects of the modern college scene.

Colleges That Change Lives (https://ctcl.org). Begun in the 1990s by retired *New York Times* education editor and journalist Loren Pope, this excellent site provides all sorts of information about searching for the right college, plus its staff attempts to dispel common myths about the college application process.

Go College (www.gocollege.com). Like College Board, Go College offers many dozens of articles covering most aspects of attending college today.

NerdWallet (www.nerdwallet.com). This useful website offers a great deal of information to young people about managing their finances, including money for college and student loans.

Princeton Review (www.princetonreview.com). Princeton Review is another invaluable general source for students, parents, guidance counselors, and others involved in the process of preparing for and attending college.

INDEX

Note: Boldface page numbers indicate illustrations.